READ ABOUT

Ancient
Egyptians

David Jay

COPPER BEECH BOOKS

BROOKFIELD • CONNECTICUT

Contents

© Aladdin Books Ltd 2000

Designed and produced by
Aladdin Books Ltd
28 Percy Street
London W1P 0LD

First published in
the United States in 2000 by
Copper Beech Books,
an imprint of
The Millbrook Press
2 Old New Milford Road
Brookfield, Connecticut 06804

ISBN 0 7613 1170 X
Cataloging-in-Publication data is on file at
the Library of Congress.

Printed in Belgium

Editor
Jim Pipe

Historical Consultant
Dominic Montserrat

Series Literacy Consultant
Wendy Cobb

Design
Flick Killerby Book Design and Graphics

Picture Research
Brooks Krikler Research

A Land of Mystery

Ancient Egypt has always amazed people. It was a land of hidden tombs, golden treasures, and scary animal gods. But what were the people who lived there really like?

Today, we know a lot from the things found in their tombs. We can also read their writing. But there is still something special about the ancient Egyptians (say "ee-jip-shans").

People are often a bit scared by mummies. They still wonder at the great pyramids built 5,000 years ago. If you'd like to know more about the amazing Egyptians, read on!

Egyptian patterns are still very popular. They were even used on the famous ship *Titanic*.

People of the Nile

The River • Floods • Working Together • Kings

The Nile is the longest river in the world, but the ancient Egyptians just called it "the river." It gave them all their water and food.

When the Nile flooded each year, the waters covered the desert with black mud. To the Egyptians, the mud was a gift from the gods. Without it, they couldn't grow their crops.

The ancient Egyptians planned their lives around the flood. Their year was divided into the flood season, the growing season, and the dry season.

In the growing season, farmers made animals push seeds into the mud with their feet.

In the dry season, the farmers built ditches. These carried the Nile waters across the land and helped the farmers to grow more food.

Most Egyptians lived along the Nile. Few people lived anywhere else because it was just desert.

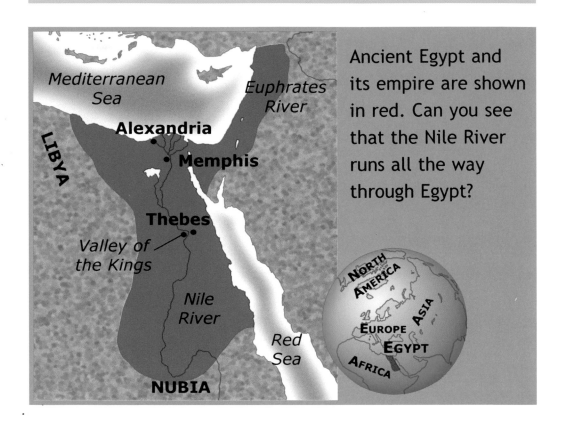

Ancient Egypt and its empire are shown in red. Can you see that the Nile River runs all the way through Egypt?

The Egyptians had to work together to build the ditches. So they created a strong leader, who was called a pharaoh (say "fair-row"), or king.

When one pharaoh died, one of his family became king. Some families ruled for hundreds of years. The Nile helped the pharaohs build a strong country — ancient Egypt lasted for over 3,000 years.

The pharaohs and the people were proud of what they did. That's why they left behind thousands of pictures of themselves, covered with lots of carved writing.

In the end, the ancient Greeks took over Egypt. Later, the Romans shut down all the temples and kicked out the priests — the last people who could read Egyptian writing.

For over 1,500 years, no one could read this ancient writing. The secrets of ancient Egypt were lost to the world.

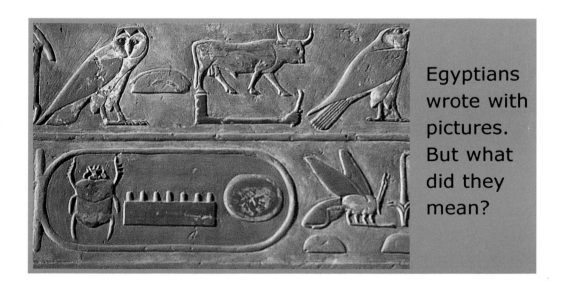

Egyptians wrote with pictures. But what did they mean?

Digging Up Egypt

Hidden Treasures • Reading Egyptian Writing

Collectors explored inside pyramids.

Nearly 200 years ago, the French emperor Napoleon attacked Egypt. He brought Egyptian experts as well as soldiers to the area.

One day, they found a black stone with three kinds of writing on it — two kinds of the Egyptian language and one in ancient Greek.

After fourteen years, a smart young French-man, called Champollion, figured out how to read Egyptian writing. Now people could find out what the ancient Egyptians had written.

Collectors took objects from ancient Egypt back to museums. Then came archaeologists (say "ar-key-yollo-jists"), people who study the past by digging up ancient things.

Their greatest find was the tomb (the burial place) of the boy king Tutankhamen (say "too-tan-ca-men").

Seventy years ago, an English team started to dig for it. The team was led by Howard Carter.

Tutankhamen's gold mask weighs more than 20 lbs.

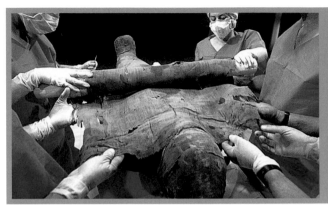

When pharaohs died, their bodies were wrapped in bandages. We call these bodies "mummies."

After two days, a boy found a step beneath the sand. Soon, they had opened up a room. Here, Carter saw "strange animals, statues, and gold — everywhere the glint of gold."

Finds like this helped to tell us what the ancient Egyptians were like. It's lucky for us that the Egyptians buried so much with them when they died.

The Egyptians built wonderful furniture out of wood. Many pieces survived in hidden tombs.

Egyptian People

Pharaohs • Scribes • Craftspeople • Women

A pharaoh was very powerful. To Egyptians, he was both a god and a human. He could speak to other gods and make the floods happen. Most people could only talk to the gods using priests.

Women didn't usually become pharaohs. Queen Hatshepsut was a female pharaoh, but she was shown in pictures wearing a beard and was called "His Majesty."

A pharaoh had one main queen and a few minor ones. Some pharaohs married their sisters.

Queen Hatshepsut's temple is still one of the most beautiful buildings in the world.

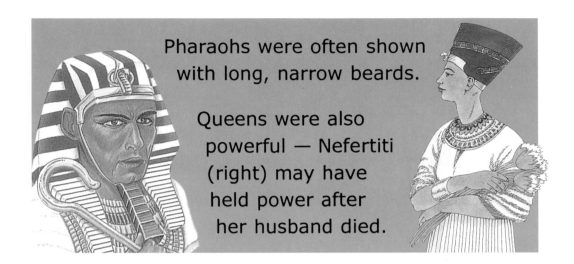

Pharaohs were often shown with long, narrow beards.

Queens were also powerful — Nefertiti (right) may have held power after her husband died.

The pharaohs also had concubines. Concubines were like wives, but they weren't as important. The pharaoh Ramses II was said to have had a hundred concubines and a hundred children.

The best jobs, like those of priests, generals, and ministers, went to the pharaoh's family or clever people chosen by the pharaohs.

Scribes (people who could write) could get good jobs. Good jobs were collecting the taxes, running building sites, or making sure the army had all the things it needed.

Next down came the craftspeople. They did beautiful work in stone, metal, wood, and clay. They made furniture, pots, wall carvings, and jewelry which are still in style today.

There were no lawyers in ancient Egypt. In court, people had to defend themselves.

Lowest down were the farmhands. They also worked as builders on the huge temples and pyramids. People were paid in cloth or food (usually bread or beer).

Rich Egyptians had a few slaves to help them in the house and on farms. They also used dogs for hunting. Some even trained baboons to pick fruit from the trees.

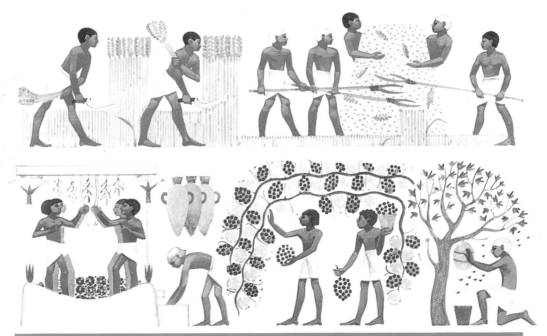

Egyptian wall paintings show us how they worked. What is happening here? Answer on page 32.

Women ran the homes, helped on the farms, and did weaving by hand. Some women also worked as singers and dancers.

Women in ancient Egypt could also own land and leave their husbands if they wanted to. This was more than women in most modern countries could do just a hundred years ago.

This woman shows how the Egyptians ground grain to make flour, like the ancient statue below.

Egypt at War

The Egyptians were not very interested in fighting. But from time to time, Egypt went to war. It also fought with itself. At first there were two Egypts — Upper Egypt to the south and Lower Egypt to the north.

Menes' crown

Under pharaoh Menes, the two Egypts became one. Menes wore a double crown, a white one for Upper Egypt and a red one for Lower Egypt.

Egyptian soldiers fought with bows and small axes.

The Egyptians also sailed north up the Nile into the Mediterranean Sea. They called it "the Great Green." Traders also sailed nearly all the way down the east coast of Africa.

Later, Egypt fought with Libya to the west and Nubia to the south (can you find these on page 6?). At times they ruled Nubia. They even ruled over land as far away as the Euphrates River in Asia.

Later pharaohs fought in chariots. Most chariots had two people in them. Why? The answer is on page 32.

D a i l y   L i f e

Egyptian houses were made of mud brick, with wooden roofs covered with plaster and palm branches. Most houses had just one or two rooms, but rich people had large villas.

Houses had very thick walls and small, high windows to keep the sun out. This kept the houses cool.

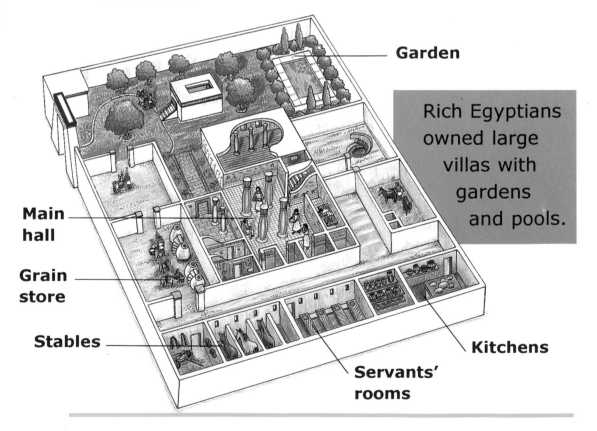

Garden

Rich Egyptians owned large villas with gardens and pools.

Main hall

Grain store

Stables

Kitchens

Servants' rooms

18

Wooden headrests, used like a pillow, were among the few items in most Egyptian homes.

Though the rich often had beautiful furniture, most people only had a few wooden stools and chests to store their things in.

In towns, the houses were often narrow and tall. The streets were dusty, noisy, and crowded.

Craftspeople lived in simple houses like these.

Here, market stalls sold everything from cloth and animals to pots and pans. There was no money so people just swapped goods.

Food was often cooked outside the house using sticks and animal dung as fuel. It probably tasted quite good.

Farms provided fruit and vegetables as well as meat, milk, and cheese. People also fished in the Nile and hunted wild animals and birds.

Rich Egyptians loved parties. At a feast there might be musicians, jugglers, and dancers.

The Egyptians enjoyed sweet pastries and cakes. They also had at least a dozen different types of beer (which was as thick as porridge).

Most of the time, women wore white linen dresses, often tight-fitting and with folds in the cloth. Men wore short skirts around their waists.

Egypt's women loved makeup and jewelry. They wore black eye-liner to make their eyes seem larger. Egyptian women liked to keep very clean and used special soap and oils.

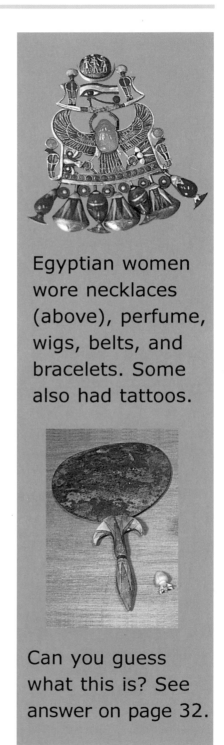

Egyptian women wore necklaces (above), perfume, wigs, belts, and bracelets. Some also had tattoos.

Can you guess what this is? See answer on page 32.

Some people shaved their heads to keep cool. Others had long hair with beads or curls. Children had shaved heads — except for a single lock.

Only rich boys went to scribe school. Other boys worked in the fields or learned a trade. Girls helped at home. Children often had animal names, such as "Frog," "Monkey," or "Hippo."

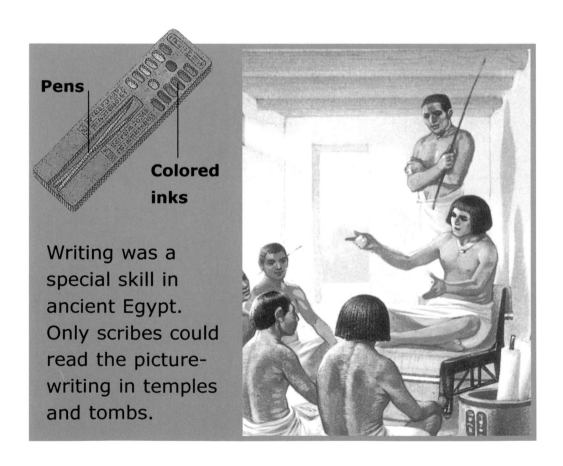

Pens

Colored inks

Writing was a special skill in ancient Egypt. Only scribes could read the picture-writing in temples and tombs.

Gods and Tombs

Gods • Temples • Pyramids • Tombs • Mummies

Religion was very important to the ancient Egyptians. Every part of their lives was ruled by a different god. If they wanted happiness, they prayed to the cat goddess, Bastet. If they were sick, they might pray to the god Anubis.

Amon Re, Sun god	Sobek, God of Water	Isis, Goddess of Women	Bastet, Goddess of Happiness

The Egyptians drew many of their gods with animal heads and human bodies. The type of animal showed what kind of god it was. Sobek, who was the god of water, had the head of a crocodile (which lives in a river).

Most Egyptians prayed at home and at holy places outside. Every town also had a temple where priests prayed to the gods.

The most important link to the gods was the pharaoh. The Egyptians believed that he was the son of the sun god, Amon Re.

Only the pharaoh could make the sun rise each day, and only he could make the waters of the Nile River flood the land.

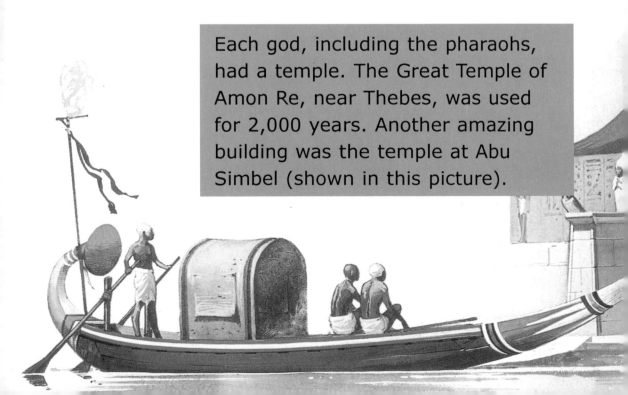

Each god, including the pharaohs, had a temple. The Great Temple of Amon Re, near Thebes, was used for 2,000 years. Another amazing building was the temple at Abu Simbel (shown in this picture).

The Great Pyramid at Giza was made of 2.6 million blocks of stone. It took 23 years to build.

Because the pharaoh was so important, the Egyptians wanted him to continue helping them after he died. They built tombs and filled them with all the things the pharaoh would need in the next world.

So pharaohs had not only temples but huge tombs where they were buried. The most famous tombs are the pyramids.

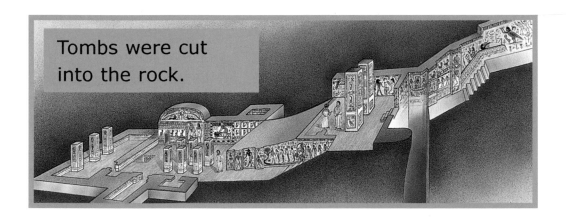

Tombs were cut into the rock.

Because of robbers, later pharaohs had their tombs cut into cliffs. Many of these tombs were built in the famous Valley of the Kings (see map on page 6). But robbers still found many of the secret tombs.

Egyptians also believed in all kinds of magic. They carried charms and used spells.

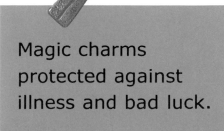

The Egyptians thought that when they died they would go to a better world.

Magic charms protected against illness and bad luck.

The ancient Egyptians wanted to keep the dead bodies in good shape for the next world. That's why they turned dead people and animals into mummies.

Priests took out the insides, dried the bodies, and wrapped them in hundreds of yards of cloth soaked in a sort of glue.

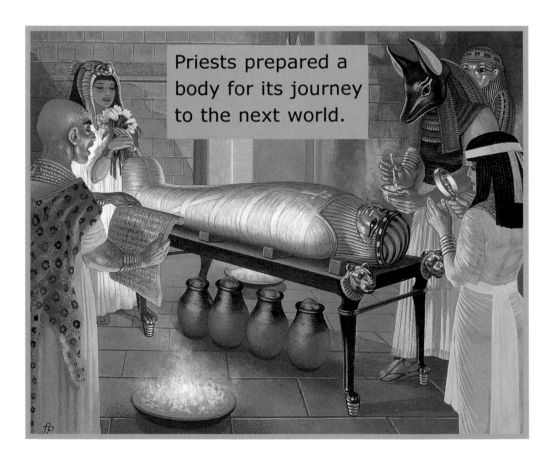

Priests prepared a body for its journey to the next world.

Canopic jars

The priests stored the inside parts of the body in special jars, called canopic jars.

The dead took with them everything they needed for their journey. For a pharaoh, this meant lots of servants (usually models), food, clothes, and furniture.

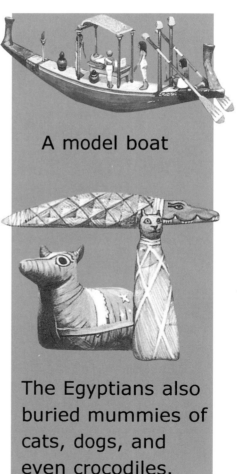

A model boat

Tutankhamen took with him 30 types of wine, 100 shoes, 30 boomerangs, and the world's first sofa bed.

Mummies and other objects tell us a lot about how the ancient Egyptians lived. But there are many other mysteries still to be solved!

The Egyptians also buried mummies of cats, dogs, and even crocodiles.

Find Out More

We know a lot about the Egyptians from their tombs. Can you name five things you might find in an Egyptian tomb? Below are a few pictures from the book, which should give you some clues. The answers are on page 32.

UNUSUAL WORDS

Here we explain some words you may have read in this book.

Archaeologist (ar-key-yollo-gist) Someone who discovers things about the past by digging up the ground to look for old buildings or objects.

Canopic jars Priests put the inside parts of a mummy into these special jars.

Mummy A dead body wrapped in bandages and stuffed with chemicals to make it last. The word "mummy" means tar in Arabic, as people once thought that mummies were covered in tar.

Pharaoh The Egyptian king. To the ancient Egyptians, the pharaoh was also a god, the son of the sun god Amon Re.

Pyramid A building with four triangular sides that meet in a point at the top. The first pyramids were built in steps. Later, the Egyptians built pyramids with smooth sides.

Scribes People who had been taught to write. They often got good jobs in ancient Egypt.

Temple A building where the priests prayed to the gods.

Tomb A special building where dead bodies are buried. Some tombs are above the ground, others are cut into the rock.

Popular Pyramids

The pyramid shape of the ancient Egyptians is still very popular. This glass pyramid is part of the famous Louvre Museum in Paris, France.

FAMOUS EGYPTIANS

Cleopatra

Perhaps the most famous Egyptian pharaoh was the last — Cleopatra, a Greek (below). She was known for her great intelligence and charm. She tried to use this to stop Rome from taking over Egypt — but failed.

Ramses II

This pharaoh (left) was a great soldier and builder. He died when he was 90, after reigning for 67 years.

Khufu

This early pharaoh built the Great Pyramid at Giza about 5,000 years ago. He was buried with a whole ship.

Who Came First?

Egyptians	Greeks	Romans	Vikings	Present Day
4,000 years ago	2,500 years ago	2,000 years ago	1,000 years ago	

Index

ANSWERS TO PICTURE QUESTIONS

Page 14 The workers above are harvesting grain. The workers below are collecting grapes and crushing them to make wine. The man on the right is collecting honey.
Page 17 It took one man to drive the chariot, and one man to fight.
Page 21 It's a bronze mirror.

Page 30 The things you might find in an Egyptian tomb are: Golden mask, human mummy, animal mummies (such as cats, birds, and crocodiles), furniture (such as chairs, beds, and tables), models of servants, food and wine, clothes and shoes, and models of ships.

Illustrators: Pete Roberts – Allied Artists, Stephen Sweet – SGA; Gerald Wood, Ivan Lapper, Mike Lacey, Peter Kesteven, and Dave Burroughs. **Photocredits:** *Abbreviations: t-top, m-middle, b-bottom, r-right, l-left, c-center.* Pages 1, 5, 7, 9, 21r & 26 – Spectrum Colour Library; 15 – Eye Ubiquitous; 11 & 31 – Frank Spooner Pictures.